# The Dragon King and his unexpected lover

Alastor gave the Novel title "The Dragon King and his Unexpected lover"

Alastor Afton

ISBN 978-93-5610-952-0

Published in India 2022 by Pencil

**Contributors:**
Co-Author: Thera Snyder

*A brand of*
One Point Six Technologies Pvt. Ltd.
123, Building J2, Shram Seva Premises,
Wadala Truck Terminal, Wadala (E)
Mumbai 400037, Maharashtra, INDIA
**E** connect@thepencilapp.com
**W** www.thepencilapp.com

## Author biography

Hi, My name is Alastor! I am a young transgender book writer I love writting! it helps me get my mind off of thing a lot you know? I personally think that writting and art can help MANY kids with copping with stress and writting is a fun way to express creativtiy! who knows maybe the will become well known for there AMAZING work of arts

# CONTENTS

# Epigraph

Don't listen to certain people, you may never know what could happen later on if you do listen to that certain person and if you DONT listen to that person who knows? Maybe you will have encounters with REALLY intresting thigns if you dont listen, sometimes its always good the break the rules you may never know what could happen

# Foreword

A book that is on 2 people who were friends since toddlerhood and then once they became teenagers they started a family and then eneded up getting married after graduating highschool

# Preface

The book on 2 childhood friends who get married later on in life

# Acknowledgements

This book includes, LGBTQ+, And slight homophobia I made this book because I want it to HOEPFULLY educate those of who are unaware of what LGBTQ is

# Introduction

So Kai, is a 6 foot 11 Radio demon who is a mafia boss and has a short wolf male hair cut with black hair and hetocromia and his left eye is light yellow and his right eye is a rose gold color with deer antlers as horns and and a imp like tail who also happens to be VERY muscular , and who has a husband, Hail and has 10 kids but they dont come in till later in the story, Hail Is 5 foot 9 and the king of white dragons and they were friends since 3 years old and ended up getting married at 18 and 20 and become eternal soulmates and Kai has 14 siblings and hes the eldest one out of the quintuplets and hes trans, Female to male and his youngest sibling who is Rhianna shes 10 at the moment but isnt brought till really later in the series, but Kai does have anger mangment issues when it comes to his gang which he has 2 locations for the mafia locations. 1 is in italy and thats were half of the gang is, and were the other half is in Austin, Texas which happens to be in america, But overall Kai is A AMAZING father and husband and just wants the best for his kids and hail, Angel his mother is a 15 foot dream demon who is the other daughter of Vero, Aka satan and shes pale and has long white thick hair and light yellow eyes and has your typical demon horns and tail and who happens to be potentionally the hottest lady on earth there is

# Chapter 1, When they first met

[Past Angel] alright sweetheart you ready to meet Hail?

[Past Kaitlyn/Kai] Yeah!
[Past Angel] Alright lets go
[Past Kaitlyn/Kai] Hello! my names Kaitlyn!
[Past Hail] My names Hail!
[Past Kaitlyn/Kai] Wanna go play in the backyard?
[past Hail] Sure!
[Author] They Played for hours and hours until it was time for Hail and his mom to go home
[Past Kaitlyn/Kai] awhh do you have to go so soon?
[Past Hail] yeah..But Mama says Ill be over again soon!
[Past Kaitlyn/Kai] Yay!, wait before you go -puts a hair clip in his hair- There!
[Past Hail] I love it
[Past Kaitlyn/Kai] Im happy you do but Bye Ill see you later hail!
[Past Hail] Bye Kaityln!
[Past Sierra] Oh Kaitlyn sure is a wonderful child isnt she darling?
[Past Hail] Mhm! and shes pretty!
[Past Sierra] Aw I think someone has a crush
[Past Hail] M-maybe!..
[Past Sierra] Oh Dont worry honey youll be having a bunch more playdates with Kaitlyn soon!, and were

enrolling you guys into the same school
[Past Hail] Yay! Thank you mama you're the best! I love you!

# Chapter 2, When they first Start kindergarten

[Past Dusk] Alright Sweetheart! you ready for your first big day of school?
[Past Kaitlyn/Kai] Yeah!
[Past Dusk] Alright I want you to have so much fun today!
[Past Kaitlyn/Kai] I will daddy!
[Past Dusk] Alright give daddy one big more hug before I have to go ok?
[Past Kaitlyn/Kai]-hugs him- Alright bye daddy! I love you!
[Past Dusk] Alright bye Kaitlyn, make sure your siblings dont get in trouble for me ok!
[Past Kaitlyn/Kai] Alright Bye Daddy!-Had went inside-
[past Dusk] the'yre growing up so fast angel
[Past Angel] I know dear, lets head home
[Past Kaitlyn/Kai] Hail! :D
[Past Hail] Hi Kaitlyn!
[Past Kaitlyn] wanna sit next to eachother at lunch?
[Past Hail] Sure!
-When the bell rings for lunchtime-
[teacher] Lunchtime Kids!
-they all head down to the cafeteria-
[Past Kaitlyn/Kai]-just eating her lunch-
[Past Hail]-Who isn't feeling to good- Kaitlyn I dont feel

good..
[Past Kaitlyn/Kai] lets get you to the nurses office ok?
[Past Hail] ok...-they both get to the nurses office-
[School nurse] Alright Mr.Storm your mom should be arving shortly to come pick you up ok?
[Past Hail] Ok...
[School nurse] your mother called saying she cant pick you up but she said your aunt angel could shes taking you guys out early and Kaitlyn's siblings out early
[Past Hail] Alright
[Past Angel] Hey Im here to take them out early
[School Nurse] Ok, Just need to sign this form to take em out early
[Past Angel]-signs the form- Alright lets go kids
-all 6 of them get in the car-
[Past Angel] Alright Hail you can stay the night with Kaitlyn since your mom cant get you and your dad is pretty busy as well right now ok?
[Past Hail] Yay! Thanks Aunt Angel!
[Past Angel] your welcome hun

# Chapter 3, Where it all bcgan

[Author] It was the first day of 8th grade at El mor middle school
[8th G. Kai]-has his head down on his desk-
[8th G. Hail]-sits next to him- you doing ok Kai?
[8th G. Kai] Mhm just my heads just hurting
[8th G.Hail] Oh hope you feel better
[8th G. Kai] Yeah Also can we head outside rq?
[8th G. Hail] Sure!
[8th G. Kai] Hail storm..Will you be my boyfriend?
[8th G.Hail] Y-Yes!
[8th G. Kai]-goes in for a kiss-
[8th G.Hail]-Kisses Back-
[principal] Uh uh Nope you can be gay somewhere else but not on my property 2 weeks of detention NOW !!
[8th G. Kai] Just for being GAY? WOW LADY BOLD TO ASSUME I AM,
[Principal] well you clearly are
[8th G. Kai] THERES A DIFFERENCE FROM BEING PANSEXUAL, AND GAY LADY

# Chapter 4, Detention

[8th G. Kai] Man this is stupid that we got detention
[8th G. Hail] Yeah I know this isnt fair
[principal] QUIT YOUR YAPPING!, Your generation filiths all these poor young kids minds!
[8th G. Kai] Shut up who even asked for your opinion? HM?
[Princiapl] SHUT IT, You know what! Call your mother right now!
[Past Angel] why the heck are you giving my son detention for being Pansexual and transgender?
[Principal] Well it was on my property!
[Past Angel] Jeez you bible thumpers dont learn AT ALL do you?
[Principal] OI! DONT BE RUDE TO ME!
[Past Angel] You have no idea who your messing with, do you? -had went in to her female grimp reaper form-
[Principal] Oh Mrs.Cipher!, I had no idea this was your son -bows her head afraid of the cipher family-
[Past Angel] God this is an AWFUL middle school, Kai, Hail darlings meet me in the car ok?
[8th G. Kai] Alright ma
[8th G. Hail] -follows him-
[Past Angel] IF I EVER find out you gave my son detention for NO reason, I will report this school to the

district and then you'll loose your job :)
[Principal] Yes Mrs.Cipher...-bows down-

# Chapter 5, ~HighSchOooOOl~

[H.S Kai]-being an idiot and chugging beer with his friends-

[HS Isabelle] Isnt he just a dream hail~?

[H.S Hail] Oi! That one is mine Scumbag!

[HS Isabelle] Pff As if! He is SO out of your league! Hes a CIPHER everyone is out of the Ciphers League!

[H.S Hail] You dont know that for sure Isabelle!, besides we been togethor for a while now

[HS Isabelle] Whatever F@gg0t

[H.S Hail] -throws her into the wall-Thats better!

[H.S Kai] -walks over to him- Hey babe, that tomatoe head gettin to you?

[H.S Hail] Somewhat...But she said your out of my league

[H.S Kai] Nah YOU are out of my League I don't know how but, I got lucky with the greatest man here <3

[H.S Hail] -leans into him-

[H.S Kai] -holds him- Mine

[H.S Hail] Hey babe? You going to the end of the year dance tonight?

[H.S Kai] Yeah, and I dont mind taking you to the dance *Mi Amor~*

[H.S Hail] -goes red- A-alright see you tonight

# Chapter 6, Where the Magic begins!(Aka The dance)

[Hs Kai] Spin the Bottle! Spin the bottle!

[Hs Ty]-spins it and it lands on bryan-

[Hs Hail] Have fun you two!~

[Hs Bryan]-takes Ty to the lockeroom to makeout with him-

[Hs Hail] I Heavily ship those two!

[Hs Kai] Yea I know and soon thats gonna be us once its my turn~

[Hs Hail] -tomatoe red-

[Hs Kai] -snickers-

-30 minutes later-

[Hs Kai] Ah! theres tweetle dee and tweetle dumb

[Hs Bryan] says the one who chugged 9 beers for $30

[Hs Kai] Worth it

-Kai and hail had went to the lockeroom but little did Kai know he accidently got Hail knocked up

[HS Kai] Hey Hail..Ive been meaning to ask you something for a while -gets on one knee-

[HS Hail] !

[HS Kai] Hail storm, Will you marry me?

[HS Hail] Yes!

[Hs Kai]-Kisses him-

[Hs Hail]-kisses back-

# Chapter 7,~Wedding~

[Past Kai]-Waiting up at the alter-
[Past Hitoshi]-walks hail up to the alter-
[Past Kai POV] Im the luckiest man there is marrying hail
[Presit] Mr.Cipher do you take Hail, as your husband?
[ Past Kai] I do
[Presit] Mr storm.Do you take Kai as your husband?
[Past Hail] I do
[Preist] you may kiss the groom
-they kiss-
[Past Dusk] TvT Hes All grown up hes no longer a pup anymore
[Past Angel] I know dear, hes a young adult now
[Past Dusk]-crying but happy for Kai and Hail-
[2 year old song]-had fallen asleep with her head next to snows-
[2 year old snow]-holds her-
[Past Angel] Aw look at our grandkids babe
[Past Dusk]-looks- aww there so freaking cute
[2 year old snow] I will never stop protecting sissy!
[Past Angel] there so freaking cute!
[Past Andre] My ship has finally went threw and it ended well
[Past Clover and Ty]-cheering for them and being morons at the same time]
[Past Bryan] Alright you 2 poofs let go home and celebrate

with some rummy
[Past Hail] Alright
-they all got in the car and drove home and played 8 rounds of rummy-
[Past Ty] Dang man! Kai keeps screwing up my hand!
[Past Hail] Hes been playing for A LONG time
[Past Ty] Oh well no duh! this dude kept laying down all aces like 7 times in a row!
[Past Kai]-snickers-
[Past Hail]-yawns a bit-
[Past Kai] tired?
[Past Hail] mhm
[Past Kai]-takes them both to there room to go sleep since is almost 4am-
[Past Ty and Bryan]-they both leave and go home to go sleep-
[Past Angel] I can't belive hes all grown up still! it was just like yesterday he was a little baby
[Past Dusk] I know babe, but hes happy with his life and look how far hes gotten in life
[Past Angel] as long as hes happy I'm happy
[Past Dusk] I married the sweetist woman on earth
[Past Angel]-smiles and gently kisses his cheek-
[Past Dusk]-smiles and flops his head in her lap an they fall asleep after watching a 2 1/2 hour long movie-
[Past Hail]-had texted Kai about him having to become king now since his parents are gone and thats how his mom got the thrown-
[Past Kai]-Text- Its ok baby I'll still be with you and Im gonna love you no matter what
[Past Hail]-holds the the phone and purrs-

[Author] Well, The reader should now know this book has finally been wrapped into a box and shipped!

## Chapter 8, Vacation!~

[Kai]-packing for the trip to Paris,France-
[Hail]-carrying heavy luggage-
[Kai] I got that for you babe -carries it-
[Hail] You sure?
[Kai] Mhm!, while we wait for the cab which is gonna be another 40 minutes why dont you take a nap? I'll take care of the luggage for you!
[Hail] Alright -had taken a nap-
[Kai]-Had finished packing and just waiting for a text message saying the cab arrived-
-40 minutes later-
[Kai] Hey babe wake up the cab is here
[Hail] Alright I'm up
[Kai]-opens the cab door for hail-
-they arrive at the airport and hours later they land in paris-
[Kai] Im gonna go get us settled in the hotel alright babe, -hands him his credit card- go spend as much as you want ok?
[Hail] you sure?
[Kai] Mhm!
[Hail]-had bought himself a nice crop top and some boot cut black pants-
[Kai] yeah I'm defiently a simp
[Hail]-snickers- a hot one as well
[Kai] yup -kisses his cheek-

[Hail]-purrs-
[Kai]-cracks his back and a loud thunger crack comes from it- ow
[Hail] you ok babe?
[Kai] Mhm! My back just needed to be cracked
[Hail] I bet! That was a really loud crack hun
[Kai] I know, anyway wanna go to the club thats being hosted by the gang thats here from italy?
[Hail] Oooo Sure!
[Kai] Alright I'll let carlos know were coming
[Hail] Alright!
-2 hours later they head to the club-

# Chapter 9, The club

[Kai]-sitting on the couch wearing black jeand and black dress shoes with a white dress shirt and sipping some whiskey-

[Carlos] dang, that's your manz right there? you got one hot stud

[Kai] mhm -puts the glass down-

[Hail]-on the pole dancing

[Kai]-smirks-

[Hail]-still dancing but then goes over to kai and sits on the chair arm-

[Kai]-kisses him-

[Hail]-kisses back-

[Carlos] ShiPppPPpp!!!~~~

[Hail]-snickers-

[Carlos]-starts blasting some salsa dance music-

[Kai]-salsa dances with hail-

[hail]-smiles-

[Kai]-smiles as well-

# Chapter 10, There anniversary!

[Kai]-getting ready-
[Hail]-doing so as well-
[Kai] Alright you ready hun?
[Hail]-finsihed getting ready- Mhm!
[Kai]-walks out to the car and unlocks it and opens the door for hail-
[Hail] thanks!
[Kai] Np -gets in-
[Kai]-pulls up- were here
[Hail] Ooo!
[Kai]-opens the door for hail-
[Hail] thanks hun!
'[Kai] np babe
[Kai]-pulls hails seat out for him and pushes the chair in-
[Hail]-smiles-
[Butler] would Mr.cipher like sparkling or still water?
[Hail] Still please
[Kai] Ill take still as well
[Butler] Very well then,-pours them each a glass of still water-
[Hail] you sure about this place babe? I don't want you speneding this much money on just food
[Kai] Babe its our anniversary, I will spend like one million plus dollars on you
[Hail] you sure?

[Kai] Mhm

[Hail] I married the most sweetist man on earth

[Kai]-smiles-

[Kai]-gives Hail his favorite flowers and a nice fire opal necklace-

[Hail] Aw! Thank you babe and heres your's -slides a box of pictures back when they were in highschool and 2 tickets to his favorite band-

[Kai]-smiles- I love it hun

[Butler] Alright we ready to order?

[both of them] Oh yes, -they both order-

-after there done eating-

[Kai]-just waiting for the check to come back-

[Hail] Babe! we should have split the bill! That was a really huge bill! -the food was $209.89-

[Kai] its fine babe I dont mind paying fully for the bill you know that

-after the check comes back they head back to the hotel for a relaxing night-

## Chapter 11, there relaxing Night

[Kai]-had changed into a baggy shirt and cargo pants-
[Hail]-had stealed kai's big hoodie and wearing shorts- Hey babeeee can we watch texas chainsaw massacre?
[Kai] sure, I'll go make the popcorn and the drinks what kind of soda do you want?
[Hail] Sprite!
[Kai] Alright,-gets hail a sprite and him MTN dew-
[Hail]-started the movie and under a ginat fluffy blanket-
[Kai]-back just in time for the movie to start and puts the popcorn in between them and the drinks on the dresser-
[Hail]-snuggles up with Kai-
[Kai]-holds him-
-after the one hour and twenty two minute movie was over-
[Hail]-had fallen asleep still snuggling with kai-
[Kai] Aw -moves so there both more comfortable and puts the blanket over them
[Hail]-purrs-
[Kai]-had fallen asleep as well listening to music-
-the next day-
[Hail]-wakes up- hm?..-checks the time and its 12:30pm-
[Hail]-turns his phone off and gets up-
[Hail] aw -looking at kai who's still asleep-
[Hail] ! -realizes there flight leaves at 12:59pm-
[Hail] Babe! wake up our flight leaves in 29 minutes!!

[Kai]-quickly gets ready and packed all there bags and drives them to the airport-
-after there 14hour and 35minute flight they landed in UT salt lake city-
[Kai] It feels good to be home back in the US
[Hail] Mhm!

# Chapter 12, home in the US!

[Kai]-opens the front door- Where home!
[Rhianna] Bubba!
[Aries] Father!
[Hail] feels good to be home
[Aries] Hi dad!
[Hail] Hey kiddo, did your siblings cause any mayhem while we were gone?
[Aries] Surprinsgly no
[Hail] Huh thats intresting
[Kai]-carrying both there luggages-
[Hail] you got it babe?
[Kai] Mhm!-goes to there room and unpacks there luggages and comes back out of there room-
[Hail]-fell asleep and burrying himself in kai pretty tired rn-
[Kai] sleepyhead -holds with wing-
[Andre] jeez! Get a room you two!!
[Kai] HUSH, if Hail wakes up I will not heistate to use the hose on you andre!
[Andre] Fair enough-walks off into the kitchen-
[Kai]-holds hail being a protective husbando-
[Dusk] Aw -snaps a picture-
[Kai]-glitches him and hail to there room and falls asleep cuddling with him-
[Hail]-really loves how toasty kai feels-
[Kai]-holding hail with a arm and sleeping listening to

music-
-47 hours after they woke up-

## Chapter 13, a normal chaotic day

[Kai]-looking at his [hone watching august his siter's arabelle's kid playing with rhianna-
[Andre]-chasing down karens with scapeles- COME JOIN THE CLOWN!
[Kai] Andre if your gonna say a pennywise line ACTUALLY do your good voice impression of him
[Andre]-does a good voice impression] COME JOIN THE CLOWN GEROGY!
[Andre]-chases the karen down with one of his scapeles-
[Angel] hes always stayed the same hasnt he?
[Kai] Yup -takes lollipop out of his mouth-
[Angel] bet our basement is FILLED with karen(s) and Ken(S)
[Kai] I would assume so, but hey were getting rid of those banshee 2 cent dollar wig people
[Angel] Pfft- you are defiently my kid
[Kai] No duh I am ma
[Angel]-laughing her butt off-
[Kai] what Im right aint I?-puts lollipop back in mouth-
[Clover] mhm
[Eclipse]-doing some werid dance- CaN I pUt My BaLls in yOww JawsssSs
[Kai] HAHA
[Clover] ok now that is pure gold
[Kai] mhm

[Eclipse] BaLlls in your Jawss
[River] Pfff-
[Clover]-had been recording-
[Eclipse] Im in your walls :>
[Clover]-screaming like in the "Hola Nino's!" meme-
[Eclipse] Pfff-
[Kai] Ah this is pure gold!!
[Andre] I know right
-all 5 of the start laughing-
[Cameron] yeah my older siblings are CRACKHEADS
[Selena] Yup
[Aj]-chasing his kids around who are both 8 months old-
-after hours and hours of being crackheads most of them go to sleep-
[Author] the reader should now be aware that this book has been finally done with the packaging

# Glossary

Pansexual- Loving all genders with having no prefrence of one
Gay-Liking the exact gender which is men
LGBTQ- Lesbian, Gay , Bisexual, Transgender , questioning
Marriage-,the legally or formally recognized union of two people as partners in a personal relationship
School dance, A event schools host for certain reasons

# List of Contributors

Alastor(Author)
Thera McPherson(Co-Author the one who reviewd it)
Paris Ajavon(Insparation)

# Notes

LGBTQ, Is NOT sinful love is love, and I made this book because I was striving for it to educate people that it exist and it is not sinful, to all those bibble thumpers who think it is, and YOU are valid don't forget about that ok :)

9 789356 109520

Printed by Libri Plureos GmbH in Hamburg,
Germany